THE ART OF
THE ICON

THE ART OF
THE ICON

IAIN ZACZEK

Picture selection by
Julia Brown

STUDIO EDITIONS
LONDON

Cover: Mother of God of the Passion,
Greek (16th century).

Frontispiece: St George and the Dragon
*(late 14th century). The image of St George defeating
the dragon is a metaphor for the triumph of good over evil.*

This edition published 1994 by
Studio Editions Ltd
Princess House, 50 Eastcastle Street
London, W1N 7AP, England

Copyright © Studio Editions Ltd, 1994

Design by Michael R Carter
Printed and bound in Singapore

ISBN 1 85891 178 8

INTRODUCTION

'We knew not whether we were in heaven or
on earth, for surely there is no such
splendour or beauty anywhere upon earth.
We cannot describe it to you: only this we
know, that God dwells there among men...

This glowing report was made by Russian observers in 988, after witnessing church services in Constantinople, and it prompted their master, Prince Vladimir of Kiev, to convert to the Orthodox Christian faith. Much of the impact had been created by the richness and variety of the icons on display, and these were to become an equally important facet of Russian culture.

The term 'icon' (from the Greek word for likeness or image) is loosely applied to the devotional panel paintings that were produced under the auspices of the Eastern Church. As in the West, the primary function of these pictures was to convey the main points of the liturgy to a largely illiterate congregation. For, as the fourth-century theologian, St Gregory of Nyssa, explained, 'The silent painting speaks on the walls and does much good.

This had become the chief stronghold of Christianity in the East, following the conversion of the Emperor Constantine and the Edict of Toleration (313) which allowed Christians freedom of worship. The technique and repertoire of icon painting gradually evolved in the new capital of Constantinople, although this development was severely checked in the eighth century. During the Iconoclast Controversy (726–843), the use of sacred images was condemned as idolatrous and thousands were destroyed. After this hiatus, the practice of icon painting was resumed, flourishing in the East until Constantinople fell to the Turks in 1453. The impact of Byzantine art was profound. In Italy, for example, it paved the way for the glories of the Renaissance, although these only emerged after painters like Giotto and Duccio had broken away from the restrictive stylizations of their Eastern counterparts. Instead, it was the Russians who became the true inheritors of the Byzantine tradition.

Missionary work had led progressively to the adoption of Orthodox Christianity in most Slavonic territories, bringing with it a firm adherence to the discipline of icon painting. The strength of these artistic links can be deduced from the prestige attached to *The Virgin of Vladimir*. This famous picture was actually executed in Constantinople, but was so highly revered in Russia that it came to be regarded as a symbol of the nation's faith and was eventually transferred to Moscow. Similarly, the fact that Theophanes the Greek (*c.* 1330–*c.* 1405), one of the very few icon painters to

Andrei Rublev, The Saviour (c. 1410).
Originally part of the Deesis tier in the Cathedral of the Dormition in Zvenigorod. In 1918, the painting was discovered in a shed near the cathedral.

achieve personal renown, spent the greater part of his career in Russia demonstrates that these ties were maintained over a long period.

Inevitably, Russian artists added their own mannerisms to the genre. There were distinctive schools at Novgorod and Pskov in north-west Russia, but of these were eventually eclipsed

Portable Icon Screen, Russian (17th century).
This miniature iconostasis gives a clear impression of the way
that icons were normally displayed in church.

by the rising star of Moscow. It was here that Andrei Rublev (*c.* 1360/70–1430), the greatest of all icon painters, produced his most dazzling masterpieces. In his work, there are serene, lyrical qualities that are far removed from his Byzantine sources.

Most of the pictures commissioned from Rublev would have been destined for display on an iconostasis, a large church screen partitioning the nave and the sanctuary. The layout for this was standard: in the centre were the Royal Doors, flanked on either side by five tiers of paintings, each of which had a specified theme. The top row represented the Patriarchs of the Old Testament. Beneath this, in descending order, there were tiers dedicated to the Prophets, the twelve major Feasts of the church, the Deesis group (*see* Plate 4) and local saints, (those worshipped at the church in question). On a much smaller scale, many households also had their own icons, which were given pride of place in the 'red corner' of the main room, so-called because it was the position which caught the first rays of the morning sunlight.

In spite of these attentions, it was the image rather than the artistry that was revered. Many icons, even the most famous, were overpainted when their varnish began to darken. This, combined with the adulterating influences of Western art, led to a creeping decline in the tradition of icon painting. The nadir was reached under the Communist régime, when many churches were turned into barns or granaries and their icons were lost or destroyed. However, with the nationalist impulses that are currently surfacing in Eastern Europe, it seems certain that a new generation of Russians will come to appreciate the cultural legacy of their icons.

— THE —
PLATES

PLATE 1

The Archangels Michael and Gabriel
(Before 1150)

This remarkable work reveals the art of icon painting in its infancy. Carbon dating by the University of Arizona has placed it in a time band of 857–1151, and the antiquity of the piece is confirmed by both the enamel-like quality of the egg tempera and the specialized nature of the underlying preparation. In addition, the strict frontality of the figures and the lack of individuality in their features conform with the early patterns of Byzantine painting. The style is provincial, perhaps Cretan.

In all probability, this was a monastic icon. As such, it would have been displayed on a stand during the week of the angels' respective festivals. Michael was the Captain of the Heavenly Host, while Gabriel was the Angel of the Annunciation. Both are depicted standing on cushions. Icon painters frequently stressed the divinity of certain figures by raising their feet off the ground. This explains, for example, the stools used by the angels in Rublev's *Trinity* (*see* Plate 8) and by the Virgin in *The Deposition* (*see* Plate 14).

PLATE 2

St George
(12th century)

We tend to associate St George automati-
cally with images of his dragon-slaying
exploits, but the early icon painters also
depicted him as a foot-soldier, armed with his
sword, lance and shield. The life of the real George
is shrouded in mystery — most of the legends
about him date from the later Middle Ages.
However, his widespread popularity as a warrior
saint is understandable enough, given the military
uncertainties of the times. In Russia, George was
also revered because of the tradition that he had
been the first man to set foot in the country before
it was inhabited and had established the Christian
faith there.

This noble figure is one of the finest and oldest
examples of icon painting from Novgorod, in
north-west Russia. It was executed for the church
of St George, which was built within the precincts
of Yuriev monastery in 1119, and its dimensions
suggest that it was originally designed to be hung
on a pillar.

PLATE 3

The Virgin Orans
(c. 1224)

This monumental work represents the Virgin in the *Orans* (praying) position. Her outstretched arms, with the palms facing outwards, reflect the attitude that was assumed during certain prayers, although the pose was also common to other religions. In early versions, the medallions were often omitted, but this example includes two angels in the upper roundels and, in the centre, a depiction of the Christ Emmanuel with His arms raised in blessing. This type of image was also sometimes known as a *Platytera* (the Ample One), in reference to the hymn, 'He made your womb more ample than the heavens.'

The icon pictured here is recognized as one of the finest products of the Yaroslavl School, which, together with Novgorod and Pskov, was one of the main artistic centres in northern Russia. The colouring and the stylized stars on the Virgin's maphorion (robe) are typical of the region, while the decorative design of the red carpet is strongly reminiscent of those that were woven at Konya in the twelfth and thirteenth centuries.

PLATE 4

Deesis
(13th century)

This type of composition would have been the focal point of the Deesis tier on an iconostasis and would have been one of the most prominent paintings on the entire screen. The Deesis tier generally featured the largest paintings and this one would have been placed in the centre, just above the Royal Doors. It depicts Christ enthroned, ready to judge mankind. The Virgin and John the Baptist stand on either side of Him and open their hands to plead for mercy for the souls that are about to be judged. This intercessory role (the word deesis means prayer or entreaty) extended throughout the tier. The flanking panels normally portrayed other saints, each turning inwards towards Jesus and displaying the same gesture of entreaty. Christ is depicted as the Pantocrator or Ruler of the Universe. One hand is raised in blessing, while His wisdom is signified by the book, which usually displays a text from one of the Gospels.

PLATE 5

The Saviour
(14th century)

This striking image has been housed in the Cathedral of the Assumption in Moscow since it was built (1475–79), and was probably one of the icons commissioned by Ivan Kalita for the previous church on that site (1326). The earliest cathedral registers (1609) state that it was installed near the tomb of the Metropolitan Peter, a place that was strictly reserved for the most sacred icons.

The character of this Saviour is very much in the Byzantine mould. In the West, artists tended to stress the compassion and the humanity of Christ while, in Orthodox versions, He was portrayed as a stern, forbidding judge. His penetrating stare is highlighted by the elongated nose and the dark, heavy-lidded eyes. By the time Rublev came to paint this theme, at the start of the following century, the mood had changed. A greater sense of optimism had entered Russian life, following the victory over the Mongols at Kulikovo (1380), and his Saviour exudes a serene mysticism.

PLATE 6

The Dormition of the Virgin
(*c.* 1390)

The Dormition (literally, the 'falling asleep') of the Virgin is a major festival in the Eastern Church, celebrated on 15 August. The subject comes from one of the texts in the Apocrypha, the 'Discourse of St John the Divine'. The Virgin lies on a bier while her soul, taking the form of a child in swaddling clothes, is cradled in Christ's arms. In the foreground, the apostles weep over her corpse, and they are joined by two bishops, St James the Less and St Hierotheus of Athens. The buildings in the background represent Jerusalem.

This particular Dormition was painted on the reverse of *The Virgin of the Don* (*see* Plate 25), an icon that was second in renown only to *The Virgin of Vladimir*. Miraculous powers were ascribed to it and the painting was sent as a talisman with the Russian army on the Livonian campaigns of 1563. Similarly, in 1591, Boris Godunov (later Tsar of Russia) firmly believed that it was responsible for preserving Moscow from the Tartar hordes of Khan Kazy-Girey. The icon was originally commissioned for Kolomna cathedral and has been attributed tentatively to Theophanes the Greek.

PLATE 7

School of Theophanes the Greek
The Transfiguration (*c.* 1403)

The Transfiguration is one of the most important festivals in the Orthodox calendar,
celebrating the moment when Christ re-
vealed his divine nature to three of the disciples.
This dramatic composition follows the narrative of
the gospels. Christ is depicted at the moment of
His Transfiguration, conversing with Moses and
Elijah. These two prophets are also shown in the
miniature *grisailles* in the upper corners of the
painting. Below, Peter, James and John fall back,
dazzled by the radiance of Christ's apparel and
terrified by the voice which booms out of a cloud
saying, in the words of Matthew's Gospel, 'This is
my beloved Son, in whom I am well pleased.' On
the sides, the group are pictured climbing and
descending Mount Tabor. The scene also features
the mystical topography that is present in so many
icons. Mountain peaks were traditionally associ-
ated with closeness to God while, at the other end
of the scale, caves symbolized the absence of
spirituality. Here, however, miniature trees are
sprouting from the darkness, mirroring the efforts
of mankind to grow nearer to God.

PLATE 8

Andrei Rublev
The Trinity (*c.* 1411)

This majestic painting is Rublev's best-known work and, arguably, the most famous of all Russian icons. It depicts the episode in Genesis when three men appear to Abraham in the grove of Mamre. Recognizing them as embodiments of the Trinity, he offers them hospitality, bringing them water, bread and meat. They, in turn, reward him by announcing that his aged wife Sarah will bear a son.

The existence of the Trinity had been acknowledged at the second Ecumenical Council (381), but its precise nature remained a constant source of controversy in the East. Accordingly, this subject, which is virtually unknown in the West, was frequently depicted by icon painters. Earlier versions – often including Abraham, Sarah and the sacrificial calf – tended to be rather cluttered, but Rublev stripped the composition down to its bare essentials. The oak of Mamre (a symbol of the Tree of Life) is retained in the background while, nearer us, the three angels gaze solemnly at the chalice on the table, which foreshadows the Eucharist, the emblem of Christ's sacrifice.

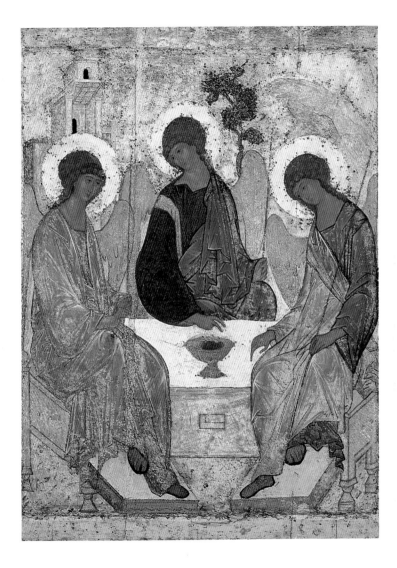

PLATE 9

The Saints Paraskeva Pyatnitsa, Gregory the Theologian, John Chrysostom and Basil the Great
(15th century)

The three male saints depicted here were the leading doctors of the Greek Church and were often shown together. In addition to their individual Feast days, they were commemorated jointly on 30 January and 12 February. Gregory (329–389) was a native of Nazianzus in Cappadocia, Asia Minor, serving there for a time before becoming bishop of Constantinople in 380. His discourses on the nature of the Trinity earned him the title of Theologian. Like his friend and colleague, Basil (*c.* 330–379), he argued fiercely against the Arian heresy, one of the major theological debates of the time about the nature of the Trinity. Basil was made bishop of Caesarea in 370 and did much to organize the principles of monastic life in the East. John Chrysostom (*c.*347–407) was renowned as a preacher and became archbishop of Constantinople in 398, before being deposed and ending his life in exile. Paraskeva was the patroness of trade and the personification of Good Friday.

PLATE 10

Battle between the Novgorodians and the Suzdalians

(c. 1460)

Historical events rarely featured in Eastern religious painting, but this exception illustrates the story of a 'wonder-working' icon. In 1169, the Novgorodians came under attack from superior Suzdalian forces. The invaders were eventually repelled and credit for the victory was given to the palladium of the city, the icon of *The Virgin of the Sign*. This icon still exists and is comparable in format to the upper half of *The Virgin Orans* (*see* Plate 3).

The miracle is depicted here in three scenes. In the upper segment, the icon is carried in procession across the river Volkhov to Novgorod. There, it is placed on the parapets as a mark of protection. Unwisely, the Suzdalian archers aim their fire at it. According to one version of the legend, the Virgin then turned towards the city and wept bitter tears; according to another, she cast the Suzdalians into darkness, giving the advantage to the defenders. This heavenly assistance is emphasized in the third section, where the Novgorodian forces are led by Alexander Nevsky, St Boris, St George and St Gleb, aided by an angel with a spear.

PLATE 11

The Entombment
(15th century)

This elegant and expressive painting combines the themes of a Lamentation and an Entombment of Christ. As with *The Deposition* (*see* Plate 14), it has been suggested that the artist belonged to the North Russian school of Kargopol, which had been colonized by Novgorod. Others have argued forcibly that the icon is an early work by Dionysius (*c.* 1430/40−1508). He was the first layman to make a name for himself in this field, with pictures that are notable for their graceful, elongated figures. There are, in addition, some affinities with Western art and it has been claimed that the painter may have been familiar with Giotto's work at Padua. If so, then the Italian's influence extended no further than the emotional drama in the foreground, for the remaining details are entirely Eastern in character. In particular, the highly stylized, almost lunar landscape indicates that the artist intended to locate the holy event in a spiritual rather than a geographical setting.

PLATE 12

St Florus and St Laurus
(15th century)

According to legend, these two saints were brothers, who interceded with the Archangel Michael on behalf of some herdsmen who had lost their horses. Their entreaties were answered and the missing animals were immediately located. Depictions of this miracle were extremely popular with icon painters, providing them with one of their most visually attractive themes. The composition here is quite conventional. The brothers are pictured at the top, on either side of Michael, who is holding the reins of two horses. Below, the missing horses are rounded up by three grooms, Speushippos (horse scout), Elashippos (horse breaker) and Melashippos (black horse).

Florus and Laurus were regarded as the patron saints of horse-breeding, and icons with their images were often nailed to stable-doors, to protect the owners against thieves. Their cult was widespread, reaching as far as France and Spain. However, the miracle was a medieval invention and there are even doubts about their martyrdom – they were said to have been stonemasons and to have been buried in a well.

PLATE 13

The Last Judgment
(15th century)

The depiction of a Last Judgment presented icon painters with their greatest challenge — that of compressing a complex series of images into a confined space. In this superb example from Novgorod, the composition is focused on the figure of the enthroned Christ, who supervises the judging process. Below Him, the coils of the great serpent, Satan, wind down like a huge umbilical cord, leading the damned to hell. An archangel bearing a long trident helps them on their way. In the dark circle above hell, the dead are awakened from their sleep by trumpeting angels. Their redemption has been made possible by the sacrifice of Christ — confirmed by the depiction of Golgotha (Calvary) on the right — and their rewards are illustrated in the two left-hand corners. At the top is the heavenly city of Jerusalem and, at the bottom, Paradise, symbolized by a garden, where the Virgin sits enthroned. On the right, the figure with the cross is the Good Thief. Beneath him, a red circle contains the Four Beasts of the Apocalypse described in the Book of Revelation which are also the traditional symbols of the four Evangelists.

PLATE 14

The Deposition
(15th century)

The Deposition was a traditional subject in both the East and the West, although this version has some unusual features. Joseph of Arimathaea is normally shown at the foot of the cross receiving the body of Christ rather than, as here, at the top of the ladder. Equally uncommon is the depiction of St John and Nicodemus removing the nails from Christ's lifeless form. The skull at the base of the picture reflects the belief that the Crucifixion took place above Adam's burial site, thus reinforcing the notion that Christ was the second Adam, whose sacrifice ensured the salvation of mankind.

However, the most remarkable element in the painting is the extraordinary curvature of Christ's body, which contrasts strongly with the rectilinear structure of the cross and the architecture. This stylistic refinement has fuelled suggestions that the artist was not only linked to the schools of Novgorod and Moscow, but was also acquainted with Western trends. One theory is that he belonged to the North Russian school of Kargopol (*see* Plate 11).

PLATE 15
St Nicholas
(16th century)

After the Virgin Mary, this saint was by far the most popular subject for artists. It was not unknown for any icon to be described simply as 'a Nicholas'. In addition to the portrait style adopted here, he was also depicted full-length. The main image was often enclosed in a rectangular band containing scenes from his life. The saint's features were quite distinctive, most notably the enlarged cranium, and he was usually portrayed in his white omophorion (a bishop's robe) with red or black crosses on the shoulders.

Our knowledge of the real St Nicholas is very scanty. He was a bishop at Myra in Lycia in the fourth century and may have been present at the first General Council at Nicæa (325). The posthumous legends are more colourful. St Nicholas is supposed to have saved three girls from prostitution, rescued drowning sailors and resuscitated some murdered infants who had been hidden in a brine-tub. He is the patron saint of carpenters, fishermen and children, and the Dutch form of his name (Sinte Klaas) has gradually evolved into Santa Claus.

PLATE 16

Virgin with Three Hands
(16th century)

The Virgin and Child was the most common subject for icon painters, partly because of the tradition that the first examples had been executed by St Luke. There were hundreds of variations on the theme, but the compositions still fall into three broad categories. The *Eleousa* or Merciful type stressed the maternal love of the Virgin and often showed her cheek resting against that of the Saviour. Both the *Virgin of Vladimir* and the *Virgin of the Don* (*see* Plate 25) belong to this format. The second type was the *Orans* (*see* Plate 3), while the third variant, depicted here, was the *Hodogitria* or Indicator of the Way. This was a severe, dogmatic image, with little show of human affection between the mother and the child. The Virgin is displayed in her role as *Theotokos* or God-bearer, while the Child is older and more knowing. In this example, He makes a sign of blessing and holds either an apple or a large cherry. Both were conventional symbols, referring respectively to the Tree of Knowledge or the Fruit of Paradise. The Virgin's three hands signified the mystical nature of the Trinity and suggest that the painting may have been destined for a church of that name.

PLATE 17
The Raising of Lazarus
(1611)

The subject of Lazarus is relatively uncommon in Western art, but it featured regularly on the Festival tier of iconostases. The episode was narrated in St John's Gospel and was of particular importance, as it prefigured Christ's own triumph over mortality. After listening to the complaints of one of the dead man's sisters, He commented, 'I am the resurrection and the life: he that believeth in me, though he were dead, yet shall he live.' Significantly, the Feast day is celebrated on the Saturday before Palm Sunday.

The composition of this Greek icon from Epirus is similar to the versions found in Russia. Mary and Martha prostrate themselves at Christ's feet, while a young man removes the cerements (burial cloths) from their brother. His tomb is positioned vertically in a cave and his halo reflects the enlightenment of the new life bestowed on him by the Saviour. To the left, we see the apostles and, in the background, the Jews of Bethany who have come to witness the miracle. Some icon painters also included a figure holding his nose at the stench from the four-day-old corpse.

PLATE 18

The Ascension of Elijah
(*c*. 1650)

The prophet Elijah was a popular subject with icon painters and he was normally portrayed either as an ascetic in the desert, where he was miraculously fed by ravens, or, as here, being transported to heaven in a chariot of fire. Some painters conveyed this image by encasing the carriage in a red globe, but this Pskovian artist has produced a more subtle effect by transforming the vehicle into an amalgam of angelic wings and flames. The figure on the right is Elisha, who is, quite literally, assuming the mantle of his master. This was the garment with which the prophet had divided the river Jordan, by smiting it upon the waters, and his protégé was able to repeat this miracle later. Elisha's inclusion is essential to the picture, for, according to the Second Book of Kings, he had asked Elijah to confer his spirit upon him and the latter had replied, 'Thou hast asked a hard thing: nevertheless, if thou see me when I am taken from thee, it shall be so.' Elijah's fiery ascent linked him with the cult of Perun, the Slav god of thunder.

PLATE 19
The Last Judgment
(17th century)

This Russian icon of the Last Judgment makes an interesting comparison with the earlier version from Novgorod (*see* Plate 13). Some of the more compelling iconographical features have been removed, but this is compensated by the greatly increased clarity of the composition. Here, the three aspects of the Trinity are enthroned together in the upper segment of the painting. The Virgin sits at Christ's right hand and the apostles are also present, fulfilling the prophecy of St Luke's Gospel that they will be judges. Beneath this, the angels sound the last trump and 'gather together his elect from the four winds', as foretold by St Matthew. These are assembled in neat ranks and include prophets, martyrs, saints and bishops. At the base of the picture, the damned are herded into a lake of fire, while the righteous arise from their tombs to witness the Day of Judgment. On the far left, some of them of are already ascending to the holy city, the new Jerusalem.

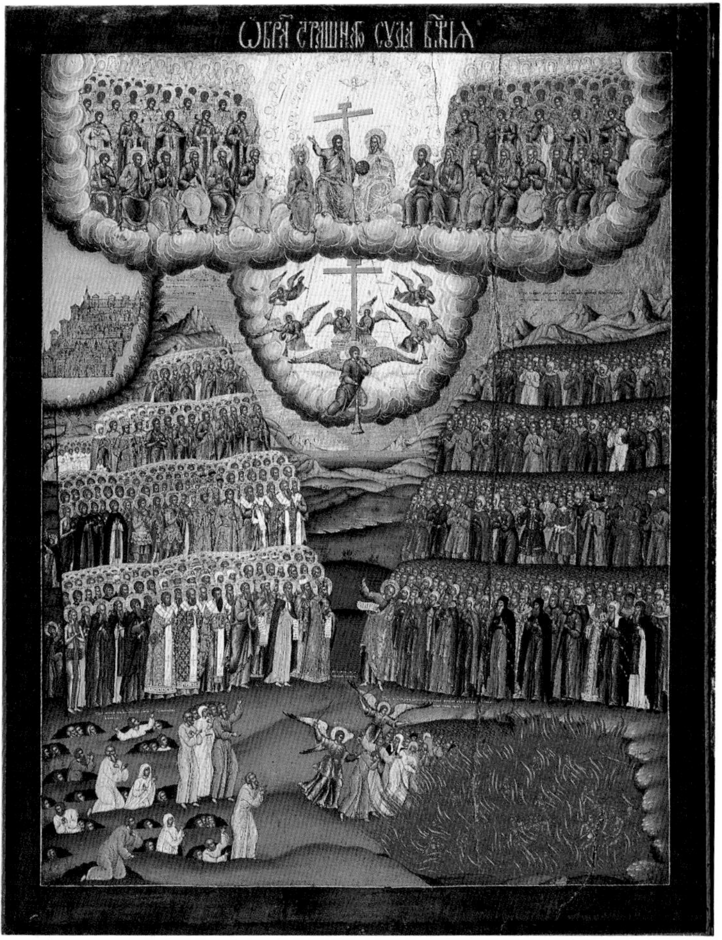

PLATE 20

The Annunciation
(17th century)

Scenes of the Annunciation capture the moment when the Archangel Gabriel appeared before Mary and greeted her, according to St Luke, with the words, 'Hail, thou that art highly favoured, for the Lord is with thee: blessed art thou among women.' The Immaculate Conception was a key element in the Christian faith and the episode inspired many painters in both the East and the West. However, after the Renaissance, their respective approaches to the subject varied considerably. Western artists tried to portray the Annunciation as a real event, with carefully modelled figures placed into believable architectural or landscape settings. Icon painters, meanwhile, felt that the spirituality of the occasion could be better expressed symbolically, without recourse to naturalism. Here, in this somewhat archaic Greek icon, the arrival of the Holy Ghost is represented by the dove, while the triple points of the divine ray of light signify the Trinity.

PLATE 21

Procopius Chirin
St John the Baptist
(17th century)

John the Baptist is depicted here as the Angel of the Desert, a theme which grew in popularity after the middle of the sixteenth century. One reason for this may be that John was the patron saint of Ivan the Terrible (ruled 1533–84), whose birthday fell on the Feast day commemorating the saint's beheading. However, the allusions here are not to John's martyrdom, but to his role as a wandering preacher. The staff in his hand signals that he has travelled a great distance, while the infant in the chalice is a token of the new life that can be gained through Christ. In the background, the tree with the axe recalls the Baptist's message, as recorded in St Luke's Gospel, about the coming judgment and the need for repentance: 'And now also the axe is laid unto the root of the trees: every tree therefore which bringeth not forth good fruit is hewn down, and cast into the fire.' In keeping with normal icon practice, the scale is governed by spiritual rather than natural laws and the disproportionate size of the saint reflects his importance.

PLATE 22

The Death of the Just Man
(1817)

The identification of this bizarre subject was made in the eighteenth-century *Painter's Manual* by Dionysius of Fourna. In this Greek icon from the Cyclades, the just man is stretched out on his back, dressed in mean attire and lying in humble surroundings. His arms are usually folded across his chest and, in some cases, the Archangel Michael smiles down approvingly at him, as he extracts the soul from his mouth. These features are intended as a contrast to the traditional companion piece, *The Death of a Sinner*, where the deceased is lying on a magnificently draped bed. The attendant demon confirms his lack of worth, however, and there are usually pictorial hints of the torments that are to come.

The Archangel Michael was commonly represented in both the East and the West as a judge of the dead, and he was sometimes depicted bearing a pair of scales. His decisions could be swayed by divine appeal, however, and an alabaster carving in the Victoria & Albert Museum, London, shows the Virgin depositing her rosary on one of these, to tip the balance in an individual's favour.

PLATE 23

Christ the Vine
(18th century)

This richly decorated panel forms the left-hand wing of a diptych. It depicts a comparatively unusual theme which developed in the fifteenth century as an illustration to a passage from St John's Gospel: 'I am the true vine and my Father is the husbandman. Every branch in me that beareth not fruit he taketh away ... Abide in me, and I in you. As the branch cannot bear fruit of itself, except it abide in the vine; no more can ye, except ye abide in me.' These words were addressed to the disciples, and they can be seen in the roundels formed by the vine and the clusters of grapes.

The other half of the diptych shows the more conventional theme of the Tree of Jesse, which relates to an Old Testament prophecy about the lineage of King David. Its composition is broadly similar. The Virgin is enthroned over the recumbent figure of Jesse and two rows of prophets mirror the arrangement of the apostles in this scene. The sumptuous design of the icon suggests a master who was familiar with the Cretan tradition and who was probably working in Corfu, in the Ionian Isles.

PLATE 24
St John on Patmos
(18th century)

As one of the Evangelists, John was a
favourite subject with icon painters and
the four disciples were often pictured
together on the Royal Doors, at the centre of an
iconostasis. He is usually shown as a young man,
participating in the events of Christ's life, but
there are also depictions of him in later life, when
he was exiled on the island of Patmos. There,
according to tradition, he received the vision of the
Apocalypse which formed the basis of the Book of
Revelation. The present icon illustrates the trans-
mission of this vision. The saint is shown in the
centre of the picture, listening to the Word of God
and dictating to his scribe, Prochorus, above
whom are depicted scenes from the Apocalypse.
In the opposite corner is St John's traditional
symbol, the eagle, which was often depicted with
a quill in its mouth, to signify the Evangelist's
authorship of Revelation.

PLATE 25

The Virgin of the Don
(19th century)

This icon takes its name from the painting on the reverse of *The Dormition of the Virgin* (*see* Plate 6). The original picture was reputedly carried on to the battlefield at the crucial victory of Kulikovo (1380) over the invading Mongols, and was named after the triumphant general, Grand Duke Dimitry of the Don. Its reputation as a 'wonder-working' icon meant that the composition was faithfully repeated by succeeding generations of artists. Here, for example, such features as the tender pose of the Virgin, the way she adjusts the Infant's drapery, and the stars on her shoulder and brow were all derived from the fourteenth-century painting.

In other respects, this picture illustrates the decline of the icon-maker's art. It had long been the practice for icons to be displayed with decorative metal overlays. These ranged from *oklads*, highlighting the halo, to *rizas*, which covered the whole icon, apart from the heads, hands and feet. By the nineteenth century, these areas of flesh were often the only sections of the icon to be painted and the resulting concoction owed more to the talents of the jeweller.

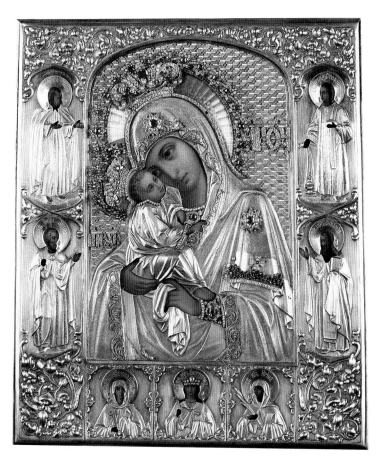

PICTURE ACKNOWLEDGEMENTS

The author and publishers would like to thank the following collectors, galleries and photographic libraries for permission to reproduce their illustrations: